LINUX
IN THE
BOARDROOM

How Linux is Changing Corporate Computing and What Executives Need to Know and Do About It.

By Mark S.A. Smith

Also By Mark S.A. Smith

Guerrilla Trade Show Selling
Guerrilla TeleSelling
Guerrilla Negotiating

LINUX IN THE BOARDROOM

How Linux is Changing Corporate Computing and What Executives Need to Know and Do About It.

© 2004 Mark S. A. Smith. All rights reserved. Reproduction of this material, in any form, is prohibited except where expressly permitted. All trademarks and registered trademarks are the property of their respective owners.

Published by
Outsource Channel Executives, Inc
12 N 33rd Street, Colorado Springs, CO 80904,
United States of America, www.OCEinc.com

ISBN 0-9749289-5-X Hardcover
ISBN 0-9749289-6-8 Soft cover
First Printing
v1.0

Printed in the United States of America.

Neither the author nor the publisher assumes any responsibility for errors, inaccuracies, or omissions. Any slights of people or organizations are unintentional.

If advice concerning intellectual property, legal, accounting, business operations, or related matters is needed, the services of a qualified professional should be sought. This publication is not intended for use as a source of technical, legal, accounting, financial, or other professional advice.

This information is not meant as a substitute for professional counsel. Neither the author nor the publisher accepts any responsibility or liability for your use of the ideas presented herein.

Some suggestions made in this book concerning business practices may have inadvertently introduced practices deemed unlawful in certain states or municipalities. You should be aware of the various laws governing your business practices in your particular industry and in your location.

Dedication

As a salute to free enterprise, this book is dedicated to all of the hard-working software engineers and designers who devote a substantial part of their life to making Linux® better, and so doing, give entrepreneurs a new choice in how they run their business.

It's also dedicated to all of the technology resellers who educate their customers on the software choices available, knowing that informed customers ultimately make the best decision for themselves, for their customers, and for the general economy.

Acknowledgements

Special thanks to Charity Andersen who believed in this project from the very start and actually made it possible.

Very special thanks to Mary Jo Wagner, a great researcher and grounded colleague.

And much gratitude to Molly Leander, the very brightest and best technology marketer that I know, and my best friend.

Contents

Introduction 2
    The Executive and the Technology Committee 2
    A Disclosure 4
    The Moving Target 4
    A Word of Advice 5
    How to Read This Book 6

What is Linux? 7
    What Linux Is 8
    What Linux Is Not 9
    Linux on the Desktop 9
    Disruptive Technology 9
    How Will You Respond? 12
    A Brief History of Linux 12
    "Free" Software 13
    What Open Source Means 14
    Open Source versus Commercial Software 16
    Linux and Industry Standards 17
    Licensing and Archiving Issues 18
    Major Linux Players 19

Contents

Linux is the Choice of Governments,
 Worldwide 21
Linux in the Courtroom 22
The Business Case for Linux 24
 Linux is Stable 24
 Linux Delivers Security 26
 Linux Brings Performance 30
 Linux Offers Flexibility 32
 Linux is Easy to Use 36
 Linux Costs Less to Buy 37
 Linux Costs Less to Operate 38
 Calculating Return on Investment 40
Where to Use Linux 43
 Where Linux Has Been Successful 44
 Add To, Don't Replace 45
 Business Applications 46
 Low-Cost Installations 46
 Consolidating Server Farms 49
 High Availability Computers 51
 Supercomputers 51
 Application Development 52
Where Not to Use Linux 54
 Replacing Windows Desktops 54
 OS-Specific Tools 56

Contents

Custom Systems 56
How to Decide if Linux is Right for Your
    Company 58
Company Direction 58
Questions for Your Technology
    Committee 60
Linux Adoption Strategy 65
    Form a Corporate Standards Committee ... 65
    Standardize the Vendors 66
    Standardize the Servers 72
    Standardize the Procedures 72
    Slowly Switch Standards 72
    Which Project to Choose First 72
Applications and Success Stories 74
Linux in Health Care 75
Linux in Finance and Banking 78
Linux in Education 81
Linux in Manufacturing 84
Linux in Retail 86
Linux in Transportation 88
Linux in Entertainment 90
Linux in Communications 93
Linux in Government 95
Appendix A - Applications 98

Contents

Office Suites 98
Groupware 100
Appendix B - Useful Web Sites 103
About the Author 105
Index 107

Linux
in the
Boardroom
How Linux is Changing Corporate Computing and What Executives Need to Know and Do About It.

Introduction

Who needs a book about a freely downloadable computer operating system? If you manage a company or if you're a part of an Information Technology (IT) decision-making team, then you need to understand the impact of Linux on your organization, your industry, and your competition.

The Executive and the Technology Committee

If you're like most executives, you're part of a technology purchasing committee. Making computer technology decisions has never been easy. You have to slog through the marketing hype and computer jargon to separate the sales-copy promises from the software reality. I remember an old saw from my software-selling days: "The difference between a used-car salesman and a software salesman is that the car salesman *knows* when he's lying."

If you're going to make smart decisions, you need to get answers to these questions:

If you're a CEO, COO, President, or Owner – How is Linux good for your operation? What does it mean to your operation and your customers? If it's going to give you an edge in the market, exactly how is that going to happen? How do you direct the people who will lead the project?

If you're a CFO or VP of Finance – Is Linux good for corporate compliance and your cash flow? Where does it fit into current regulations?

If you're a CIO, CTO, or IT Manager – Is Linux good for your computing infrastructure? How do you evaluate Linux? What should you look for in a Linux vendor? What about security?

This book was written with the non-technical manager in mind; it won't dig very deep into the technology. So, even if you're an executive with limited technical background, this book will guide you on the questions to ask and the issues to examine when your technology team considers Linux for your company.

A Disclosure

Quite frankly, this book is pro-Linux. I wrote it to help speed the adoption of Linux by presenting its benefits and discussing adoption processes in a way that executives, like you, can understand. I believe that if you're looking for ways to improve your business productivity or decrease your information technology expenses, then you should consider Linux as a part of your business strategy.

I'll discuss where I think Linux has limitations. No single software choice can satisfy all of your computing needs. Optimizing your operation means having choices and making educated decisions. For most businesses with more than 50 employees, Linux should be considered for at least some of the computing tasks.

The Moving Target

The Linux market is moving so fast, that it's highly probable that by the time this book is in your hands, details have changed. Yet the fundamental business-decision drivers won't change for several years, if not a decade.

The appendix lists Web sites where you can get the latest information on Linux and I recommend that you contact the leading manufacturers to get the latest information about their products and business solutions.

A Word of Advice

For executives, understanding whether or not Linux is a suitable choice is made far more difficult by its passionate proponents and bitter critics.[1]

Being influenced by a single manufacturer's sales rep results in myopic solutions and carries a high probability of less-than optimal results. I recommend that you select a competent, independent technology reseller who offers a range of products from a variety of software vendors to be a part of your technology advisory team.

---

[1] One slam Web site: www.linuxsucks.org

How to Read This Book

Start by scanning the first few chapters, stopping at the subheadings that catch your eye.

Then review the case study that best matches your industry or your technology situation.

Finally, consider the assessment questions on page 60 to help explore the issues with your technology committee.

What is Linux?

Linux (li' nuks) is a public-domain computer operating system[2] (OS) that is freely downloadable from the Internet. Because it's free, Linux challenges some of the biggest computer software and hardware manufacturers to rethink their business strategies. Linux proponents choose the OS because of increased stability, performance, flexibility, and efficiency.

Linux is a hardware-independent OS, and every major computer vendor offers Linux-ready servers[3] and desktop machines.

---

[2] The operating system is the base-layer software that interfaces the hardware (display, keyboard, disk drives, central processing unit, memory, and so forth) with the software that runs your business. This lets software designers ignore the hardware and focus on the functions that you want. When you "boot up" your computer, the system loads the OS so that you can then run your business applications.

[3] A server is a computer used through a network (often simultaneously by many people) as compared with a

While Linux is freely available, paid versions (called distributions) include additional tools and applications, documentation, training, and technical support. Leading technology companies, such as IBM, Oracle, and Hewlett-Packard offer technical support for Linux as part of their service offerings.

What Linux Is

Linux is an alternative to other OS's like the pervasive MS-DOS® and Microsoft® Windows® and is rapidly replacing the IT industry-standard UNIX® (such as Mac OS, IBM's AIX®, Sun's Solaris™, HP's HPUX®, and others).[4] Linux runs the Google search engine, the Amazon.com Web site, and FedEx's operation. It

---

    desk-top machine usually used by one person at a time.

[4] UNIX (yoo' niks) is the industry-standard server OS developed in the 1970's by Bell Telephone Laboratories. The Open Group holds the definition of what a UNIX system is and its associated trademark in trust for the industry. The worldwide UNIX market in 2001 was more than USD $25 billion.
www.unix-systems.org

runs on a wristwatch, PDA, and your TIVO box. It runs the International Space Station.

What Linux Is Not

Linux is not a business application like a word processor, spread sheet, or enterprise resource planning (ERP) tool. It's the software foundation that lets you use these and other computer programs that "run under" Linux.

Linux on the Desktop

It's the early days for Linux on desktop computers; there aren't many corporate solutions yet available. The future looks promising. IBM and Adobe have announced plans for Linux-based desktop applications.

Disruptive Technology

Linux is a disruptive technology: it changes everything. It revolutionizes how applications are developed, how applications are deployed, and how companies use an operating system to improve their competitiveness.

The proof of this is Linux's rapid growth despite the fact that there *is no single company* promoting Linux! At the end of 2003, Linux showed a 63.1 percent dollar volume growth year-over-year, unit shipments grew 52.5 percent year-over-year, and Linux servers generated USD $960 million in *quarterly* revenue.[5]

Linux adoption has jumped in the past several years. Industry analyst, Gartner[6] released a survey December 2003 that showed 41 percent of firms with more than 500 employees use Linux in some form. This compares with just 15 percent in the last quarter of 2001.[7] Gartner reports that 45 percent of mid-sized businesses are using or experimenting with Linux. By 2006, Linux is expected to be the predominant, or near predominant UNIX-type

---

[5] According to IDC's Worldwide Quarterly Server Tracker, February 2004. www.idc.com
[6] www.gartner.com
[7] Gartner, August 2003 as reported in CNET magazine, asia.cnet.com/newstech/systems/ 0,39001153,39145673,00.htm

OS,[8] and one of the major OS's in most enterprises.

Further proof of Linux's disruptive nature is the rancorous attacks by other OS vendors. Microsoft executives have called Linux "...a cancer..."[9] and UNIX vendor, The SCO Group, has launched lawsuits against Linux users. (More about this on page 22.)

More proof:
- 188 of the top 500 supercomputers are Linux based, more than any other operating system.[10]
- In November 2003, IBM signed their 100,000th third-party developer[11] to

---

[8] The word UNIX is not used in conjunction with Linux because UNIX is a registered trademark. Linux is a best-of--breed UNIX based on the IEEE POSIX standard. www.pasc.org

[9] See Microsoft's Linux rebuttal at www.microsoft.com/mscorp/facts/

[10] www.top500.com

[11] IBM calls them ISV's, Independent Software Vendors.

work on Linux applications and adds 2,000 more each month.[12]
- IBM has more than 7,000 employees working on Linux-related projects.[13]

How Will You Respond?

With this level of growth and support for Linux, there is high probability that Linux will be part of your company in the future. Prudence dictates that if you choose to not use Linux today, that you, at the very least, avoid decisions that limit future implementation.

A Brief History of Linux

Linux evolved from a *kernel*[14] created by Linus Torvalds in 1991 while studying at the University of Helsinki. (Linux is a contraction of "Linus's UNIX".) When the author of the UNIX version[15] Torvalds was using refused to make

---

[12] Reported in IBM's *Linux Executive Report*, February 2004. www.ibm.com/linux
[13] As of February 2004.
[14] The kernel is the essential core of the OS.
[15] UNIX versions are also called *flavors*.

suggested improvements, he created his own operating system that embraced users' comments and suggestions.

Linux does not include any UNIX code, but it is a UNIX clone, which means it offers many of UNIX's technical features.

Although Torvalds holds the copyright and trademark to Linux, he chose to make the OS available to all as *free* software.

"Free" Software

In the early 1970's, Richard Stallman, with the Massachusetts Institute of Technology Artificial Intelligence lab, pioneered the concept of free software, in the sense that *free* doesn't mean no-cost, but means *freedom to use, distribute, and modify*. He founded GNU[16] in 1984 to distribute software created out of this philosophy.[17] Stallman points out that the rule of most

---

[16] www.gnu.org

[17] Stallman's philosophy: You have the freedom to run the program, for any purpose. You have the freedom to modify the program to suit your needs. (To make this freedom effective in practice, you must have ac-

software vendors is, "If you share with your neighbor, you are a pirate. If you want any changes, beg us to make them."

Linux breaks the stranglehold on proprietary operating systems by being part of GNU's *open source* software.

What Open Source Means

Open source means that the *source code* of the program with the details of how every process and procedure works, is available to all.[18]

Open source programming community members (estimated to be more than 120,000 strong) make improvements to the software and submit them for inclusion in future re-

---

cess to the source code, since making changes in a program without having the source code is exceedingly difficult.) You have the freedom to redistribute copies, either gratis or for a fee. You have the freedom to distribute modified versions of the program, so that the community can benefit from your improvements. www.gnu.org/gnu/thegnuproject.html

[18] As part of open source compliance, even TIVO makes their source code available to the general public. See more at www.tivo.com/linux

leases. These individuals work on their own or for companies that benefit from the open source applications. Their rewards come from peer recognition and from showcasing their analytical abilities and programming prowess with their code contributions.

By some estimates, the average open-source community programmer dedicates more than 10 hours a week to the community. Some opine that this is because they can't get a date.

As an engineer, I understand the psychology of the open source community. These scientists are frustrated because they feel that too many great projects are killed by executives who don't see the immediate commercial value or from a lack of funding.

In the open source community, bright minds bring their ideas into the world without executive approval or corporate budget. The result is that Linux and other business applications in the open source libraries have early support for leading-edge technology.

A bonus: bugs are rapidly identified and fixed. It also means that Linux is tested on literally thousands of computer configurations, improving its reliability and stability.

Linux will be around for a very, very long time because the open source community holds and maintains Linux, not a corporation.

Open Source versus Commercial Software

Some companies choose commercial software because they feel that they'll have a solution that's guaranteed to work and, if necessary, they can enforce product performance through the legal system.

One look at most commercial software licenses and you'll see that most vendors don't guarantee that anything will work. Most software vendors have a no-returns policy. Once you've taken delivery, you can't give it back.

For any technology, the solution is only as good as the local people who support you. These are the people you pay to make your system work. If you find good support for

Linux, you'll be home free. And with open source, your computer consultants can actually make changes to the software, if that's what's required.

Linux and Industry Standards

Linux is based on several standards including the POSIX standard for UNIX and GNU standard for open source software releases. Most UNIX releases are based on similar standards.

Other operating systems claim to be industry standards, but that can only be true if other companies manufacture another version of the product that is interoperable. And this just isn't true with the exception of UNIX and J2EE.[19] If you want to use OS standards, choose UNIX or Linux.

Linux supports virtually all standard document file formats including ASCII, XML, HTML, SGML, LaTeX, TEX, PostScript®, and PDF.

---

[19] J2EE is the industrial strength version of Java, another open source computer language.

If your company uses Microsoft Office tools, there are Linux alternatives. Microsoft Word and Excel® file formats can be accessed and written under Linux by OpenOffice, KOffice, Saig Office, StarOffice™, and other open source applications.[20]

Licensing and Archiving Issues

If legislation or corporate policy requires your company to archive records for a certain period, then you should seriously consider open source software.

Most OS vendors now license their software for a time period instead of in perpetuity. This means that if you have a requirement to hold records for decades, you may be out of compliance when the OS is no longer supported. Access to the data becomes no longer possible, legally. With Linux, you will always have *legal* access to the software and information that your company needs. You won't be

---

[20] More about these tools in the appendix on page 99.

forced into unnecessary upgrades or be restricted by a single-source vendor.

History shows that OS vendors make substantial changes in how they maintain back-up files and even change how they store data in files from version to version. (If you've tried to restore Microsoft Windows 98 back-up files on Windows XP, you understand.) With Linux, your operation has control over how data is stored and retrieved through your data's lifecycle. This means that you always have access to old data.

Major Linux Players

More than 150 companies distribute Linux.[21] The major IT vendors have chosen to ally with one or more of the leading Linux distributions to bring comprehensive business solutions to market. Some major corporations who back Linux with products and support include: Citrix, Computer Associates, Conexant, Dell, Hitachi, HP, IBM, Mips, Motorola, NEC, Net-

---

[21] For a list of distributors, see www.linux.org/dist/

work Associates, Nokia, Novell, Oracle, PeopleSoft, Philips, Red Hat, SAP, Sharp, Silicon Graphics, Sony, Sun, SuperMicro, Sybase, Trend Micro, Veritas, and VMWare.

Virtually all of IBM's software runs under Linux. Since April of 1999, IBM Global Services has delivered 24x7 Linux support. IBM holds a USD $30 million stake in Novell, owner of SUSE LINUX. And IBM has invested billions promoting Linux, world wide. No doubt you've seen their Linux ads on TV and in print.

Oracle, the largest database company, delivers all products for Linux and offers Linux OS-level support for their customers.

Other major database providers (DB2, mySQL,[22] Informix, and Sybase) support Linux. The only one missing from this list is Microsoft.

All Hewlett-Packard ProLiant servers, blade servers,[23] and Itanium 2-based servers

---

[22] mySQL is an open source database. www.mysql.com

[23] Details about blade servers on page 39.

and workstations are available with Linux. Hewlett-Packard also ships select desktops with Linux pre-installed.

Dell offers Linux support on all servers.

Sun, a leading supplier of big servers and the inventor of Java, produces the open-source StarOffice Suite for Linux that offers business tools similar to Microsoft Office for $25.00 to $80.00 per user.[24]

Even low-cost retailer, Wal-Mart sells pre-configured Linux computers on-line for less than $300.

Linux is the Choice of Governments, Worldwide

Major country governments such as United Kingdom, Russia, China, and Brazil are accelerating their adoption of Linux to reduce their operating expenses, just like the major companies who have adopted the OS.[25]

---

[24] More details in the appendix on page 100.
[25] More about this on page 95.

The city of Munich recently replaced 14,000 Windows desktops with Linux to decrease costs, decrease reliance on a single vendor, and increase security.[26]

Less technologically advanced countries see Linux as a promising way to elevate the standard of living by providing low-cost computing, Internet access, and new ways for their people to make a living with technology.

Linux in the Courtroom

On March 7, 2003, The SCO Group filed suit claiming IBM used some of SCO's proprietary UNIX software code in the universally-distributed Linux kernel. SCO has sent thousands of letters to customers demanding licensing payments to use any distribution of Linux or risk suit.[27]

Most experts believe SCO's claims are unfounded, their evidence unconvincing, and their chances for winning improbable. The case

---

[26] www.computerworld.com/softwaretopics/os/linux/story/0,10801,71659,00.html

[27] See SCO's rationale at www.sco.com/5reasons/

hasn't seemed to slow Linux's adoption.[28] And a key reason is that the leading Linux vendors offer legal indemnification for their customers.[29]

A side note: SCO owns Caldera Linux, one of the major distributions. SCO suspended distribution until they resolve their lawsuit against Linux distributors. I guess SCO figures that there's no sense in suing themselves.

---

[28] For the status of the lawsuit, see www.linux.org
[29] For a good article on indemnification, see techupdate.zdnet.com/techupdate/stories/main/SCO_legal_train.html

LINUX IN THE BOARDROOM

THE BUSINESS CASE FOR LINUX

The greatest benefits from using Linux are stability, performance, flexibility, and lower total cost of ownership. IT executives report that open source provides greater flexibility, control, and faster, cheaper application development.[30]

Linux is Stable

Users report Linux delivers better reliability on Intel servers than Windows.[31] While Linux may not *yet* be as reliable as other flavors of UNIX, it delivers a strong price-reliability ratio because it runs dependably on lower-cost Intel hardware. If you're frustrated by your com-

---

[30] "Open Source Gains Momentum," CIO Research of 375 companies, December 2002. www.cio.com

[31] You're probably familiar with the "Intel® Inside" campaign. Intel manufactures the bulk of computer chips. Computers that use Intel devices are often lower cost than those that use chips from other companies. www.intel.com

puters going down, you can look to Linux to improve system reliability.

Increased System Stability

Linux is a proven solution where companies can't tolerate an unstable or "usually-stable" OS. Linux doesn't freeze up or slow down over time so it doesn't need to be rebooted periodically to maintain peak performance.

There are countless documented cases of a Linux-based server staying up until the operator took the system down for repairs or upgrades.

Mission-Critical Applications

Many companies are now using Linux for mission-critical applications that must be online all the time. For example, with the IBM.com e-commerce site, an outage costs more than USD $20,000 per minute! IBM runs other mission-critical applications under Linux such as support of their new USD $2.5 billion computer chip plant and applications supporting their 300,000 worldwide employees.

Maybe your business isn't that big. Businesses of all sizes, small through enterprise, have access to the same type of Linux clusters[32] that IBM uses to keep their site up all the time. There is no favoritism towards large companies because Linux doesn't require big computers or highly-trained operators.

Up-Time Upgrades

With other OS's, your IT people have to completely shut down the computer system to make upgrades and software patches. With Linux, your computer system can still be working while being upgraded.

Linux Delivers Security

Depending on your operating system (OS) to deliver computer security is naïve. Virtually every OS has been hacked. So when we talk about OS security, it's about levels of security. The most secure computer systems are unplugged from the Internet and locked behind

---

[32] More about clusters on page 51.

doors. The least secure systems are connected unprotected to the Internet with no passwords.

There are many facets of computer security, but germane for most companies are protection from unauthorized employees and defense against outside attacks.

Inside Job

More than 70 percent of computer break-ins are from disgruntled or unauthorized employees[33] and frankly, unauthorized employee security issues are pretty much the same for all OS's. The defense lies in enforced security policies, cooperation between human resources and the computer department, and computer audit trails.

Virus Strikes

When it comes to outside attacks and exploiting vulnerabilities with viruses, there are real differences in OS's. While there are viruses written for Linux, the number pales compared

---

[33] Download the latest Computer Crime and Security Survey from www.gocsi.com

with how many have been written for Windows and other Microsoft products. This means fewer attacks on your Linux system.

No doubt, virus writers will target Linux more frequently as it becomes more popular. But, even when Linux is hacked, with the avid support of the open source community, the situation is often fixed within hours of discovery, much faster than any commercially available OS. This means that vulnerabilities get patched faster.

If your server is connected to the Internet, you need protection. Several companies create anti-virus programs specifically for Linux.[34]

Linux Security

Linux systems tend to be the most secure of all operating systems from outside attack. And there are several reasons why.

Like other OS's, Linux uses a security hierarchy that governs what a user at a certain

---

[34] A leading Linux anti-virus vendor is Trend Micro. www.trendmicro.com

access level can or cannot do and sets permission for who or what can read or write to a specific file. Setting the most critical permissions requires the highest level of administrative access (called *root access*).

Linux-based programs usually don't expect or require root access, although many Windows programs do, making it easy for virus writers to take over critical system files. This means that with Linux, a virus generally cannot infect system files and "take over" a computer because of system-wide restrictions that are usually in place.

Even if a virus was introduced by one user, it usually can't affect the files of other users because of the permission structure.

Security Depends on Your Operators

While Linux is more secure than most OS's, any OS can become unsecured by computer system users. OS security doesn't help if your people have passwords written on slips of paper in their desk or give passwords out over the phone.

A computer operator can intentionally or inadvertently remove security safeguards on any OS and open it up to attack. Most system administrators who have experienced a security breach knew that they were vulnerable and hadn't done anything about it.

True for any system, your operators need to know what they're doing and follow established guidelines on configuring the computer to meet your required level of security.[35] For a secure system, create or adopt a security policy for your company, and then strictly enforce it.

Linux Brings Performance

Because Linux uses computer resources more efficiently, some companies have seen 50 to 70 percent increases in capacity by just switching to Linux.[36] This means that you don't have to

---

[35] For a series of articles on stupid security mistakes, see http://searchenterpriselinux.techtarget.com/qna/ 0,289202,sid39_gci962066,00.html

[36] As quoted in CIO magazine. www.cio.com/archive/030104/open.html

buy the latest technology to have a powerful and stable computer system.

Runs on Older Systems

Linux operates well on older computers because it doesn't need as much memory or computer power to get the same job done. That old computer that limps along under Windows will leap with Linux.

Decreases Operator Costs

Most current Linux distributions are user friendly and install and set up easily. So, expect decreases in IT operator costs. Not only are the salaries for Linux operators less than for proprietary OS's, but because of the way Linux works, a single operator can support more systems. Operators need less training and support because running a Linux application on different types of computers requires no additional instruction.[37]

---

[37] "The Total Cost of Ownership for Linux Web Servers in the Enterprise," Robert Frances Group, 2002. www.rfgonline.com

No Forced Upgrades

Most companies that have moved to open source software have experienced significant decreases in operating costs because they aren't forced to upgrade to the latest version of the software on a manufacturer's whim. This means that you aren't forced to pay increasing licensing fees or rework systems that require new hardware to support the upgrade.

Linux Offers Flexibility

Linux has matured very rapidly because of the number of open source community programmers who have worked on it. The brightest and best computer scientists contribute so Linux includes innovative features and functions that until recently were reserved for finely-tuned proprietary operating systems. Some claim that Linux gets the best stuff first.

Get the report from
www.ibm.com/linux/
RFG-LinuxTCO-vFINAL-Jul2002.pdf

With Linux, you enjoy well-tested, field-proven, leading-edge support for the computer hardware that you want to use in your organization.

Or your staff can modify the software to your own liking or fit special needs because the source code is open. Your company can add its own innovation.

Run with Linux and Another OS

Most vendors will let you run the Linux version of their application for little or no additional charge, assuming you're moving it from one computer to another. This means that you can easily move from your existing OS to Linux with current software licenses.

Linux Offers Choice

Because of the large number of companies who support Linux, you're never locked into a relationship with a single vendor. You can choose the vendor for the OS that you like best. You can then choose the vendor for the *tools* you like best. You can also choose the vendor with the best computer *hardware* for your company. Or you can buy it all from one vendor, if that's what you prefer.

This lets your team shop around for the most cost-effective solutions and change computer hardware architectures as new ones become available. With Linux, you decide what works best for your business.

A Natural Upgrade Path

Your team can test a Linux-based application on a low-cost Intel-based computer, then roll out with a more powerful platform, and ultimately scale up to operate on a mainframe, all under Linux.

This means that you can move up in computing capability sooner because the upgrade path from one platform to another is less expensive. For example, a business can begin with a simple Linux-based e-commerce package running on a no-name PC clone and, as the company grows, migrate with minimal effort to a Dell, HP, IBM, SGI, or Sun server. Linux even runs on an IBM mainframe.[38]

Consistent from Computer to Computer

Linux is computer hardware agnostic. Linux distributions are available for virtually every computer manufactured, including computers that haven't been supported for years by other OS's. Linux can often run common UNIX utilities and applications. Virtually all data file formats are supported. This allows applications to be delivered from a wide variety of computers, yet you can't tell from the user interface if the computer you're using is a PC, a workstation, or a mainframe.

This transparency prevents interruption of workflow as your computing needs change. It means that you can use almost any computer hardware to operate your system. And when you choose to add new hardware, your people

---

[38] A mainframe is a large computer often used for centralized large-scale computing purposes.

using the system won't need additional training.

Linux is Easy to Use

In the past, beginning Linux users would gripe about the difficult installation procedures and cryptic commands used to operate the system.

Today, most Linux installations are fast and easy and feature an easy-to-use graphical user interface based on a standard called X[39] that looks much like Microsoft Windows or Mac OS. Most Linux distributions come with one of the free, open source versions, most popular being KDE[40] and GNOME.[41]

Like other graphical user interfaces, you can configure the look of the desktop and customize it for your preferences.

A key difference with X is that you can operate any Linux computer over a network with X windows (with the proper authorization) whereas Microsoft Windows is much more

---

[39] www.x.org
[40] www.kde.org
[41] www.gnome.org

limited. With X, any computer on your network looks and acts like it's the local computer.

What this means is that you can have computer servers without keyboards and monitors that are all controlled by a single operator from a single location without any additional hardware or software.

Linux Costs Less to Buy

You can download Linux from the Internet for free from almost every distributor in accordance with the Linux general public license.[42] But you don't get support at that price.

Most Linux distributors make their living by providing technical support, maintaining the software surrounding the Linux kernel, and publishing the software and documentation. While the Linux kernel is technically free, you'll pay for the rest of their services, and it's worth it.

Linux distributions range from USD $50 to $20,000 depending on the type of computer

---

[42] Get details at www.gnu.org/copyleft/gpl.html

being licensed. Expect to save about 10 percent of your IT budget when you choose Linux.

Support costs and services costs still remain and will be similar to what you're paying now. You may see a reduction in support costs if, today, you have various operating systems from multiple vendors. You may temporarily incur increased costs as your people learn the new Linux-based systems. Yet, you probably bear this cost now when your current vendors release new versions, forcing your people to change procedures or learn new features.

Linux Costs Less to Operate

Beyond reducing software costs, Linux brings other savings.[43] Amazon.com moved from UNIX to Linux, cutting their technology capital budget by 25 percent.

Reduces Hardware Costs

Over the past few years, the computing power of Intel-based machines has caught up with the

---

[43] Read an article for CIO's about Linux cost savings, www.cio.com/archive/030104/open.html

mid-level servers from other vendors. Linux delivers UNIX-like reliability and power on low-cost Intel-based computers. This means that you can build servers on inexpensive machines instead of buying the much more costly hardware traditionally used for servers.

Runs on Low-Cost Blade Computers

A rapidly emerging trend is to use *blade servers* for corporate computing. These inexpensive computers-on-a-board (called blades) plug into a rack that holds multiple boards. The boards interconnect through a built-in network connection.

There's no need for a keyboard, mouse, or display for each blade because the system operator controls individual boards through the network. This means that the blade server system can be controlled from anywhere, reducing the need for on-site personnel.

When you need to add computer power, just purchase and plug in another blade instead of buying a whole new box. You don't even need to turn off the system.

Linux works well for blade computers because of its strong network support, low software cost, and widely available software supporting tasks suited for this type of environment.

Calculating Return on Investment

Consider these factors when calculating the ROI of using Linux in your operation. Some of the factors are easy to calculate, others are much fuzzier.

The Costs

- Staff training for those unfamiliar with Linux. Calculate wages, overhead, and training costs for on-line training. Add travel expenses if you select classroom-based training.
- Researching Linux vendors.
- Evaluating solution options.
- Purchase of Linux distribution (USD $50 to $20,000).
- Support for Linux.

- Required management and reporting tools that aren't included in the Linux distribution.
- Migration switching costs, including testing of the new system.

The Savings

- Increased staff efficiencies (10 to 100 percent).
- Less costly new hires when expanding (0 to 50 percent).
- Less costly staff outsourcing (0 to 50 percent).
- Potential lower OS cost when adding new computers (typically 10 percent savings).
- No software cost for common network applications like Web servers, print servers, and file servers.
- Increased capacity of Linux on existing computers (20 to 50 percent increase in capacity).
- Eliminated cost of security breaches from unpatched software.

- Reduced cost of business interruptions when upgrading current OS.
- Eliminated cost of required hardware upgrades demanded by other OS's software releases.

The Contingency Costs
- On-going availability of open source software versus escrowed software from a vendor.
- The open source community's lifespan versus a proprietary software vendor's business viability.

Depending on your plans, there are additional ROI factors to consider. For example, when consolidating server farms,[44] consider the staffing savings, power savings, and floor-space savings. Include the costs of new hardware and learning curve costs.

---

[44] More about server farms on page 49.

Where to Use Linux

In the past, Linux has typically been brought into a company by the technical staff (sometimes surreptitiously) for computing infrastructure tasks such as file servers, print servers, and Web servers. Linux has over-delivered in these roles: more flexible than expected, more reliable than expected, and costing less than expected.

Now, IT managers are asking, "Can other areas of our business benefit from the improvements in flexibility, reliability, and cost-effectiveness we've come to expect from Linux?" And that's probably why you're reading this book.

In a survey of 50 companies with Linux experience, industry analyst, Forrester Research found that 72 percent expect to run more Linux and that Linux carried every kind of workload:

Web, applications, infrastructure, and databases.[45]

Where Linux Has Been Successful

Linux excels in networked environments. Part of this is because Linux was developed by a community of programmers over the Internet, so network support is part of the design criteria. Typical network-based tasks like remote disk backup typically run faster and more reliably than with other systems.

Linux has been most popular for Web servers, where the need for reliability and consistency across computers drives the IT decisions. Eighty percent of Web sites use the open-source *Apache* Web server with Linux.[46]

The next most popular Linux application is e-mail. Many Linux-based shops use *sendmail*,

---

[45] August 2003, news.com.com/2030-1069_3-5059572.html
[46] Most Linux distributions include a copy of the Apache server software. www.apache.org

an open-source package that offers basic Web-based e-mail including anti-spam filtering.[47]

Linux is very popular for file and print serving. *Samba* is an open-source package that makes a Linux server look like a Windows file and print server.[48]

Database applications check in at fourth place with 38 percent of customers saying they're deploying a database on Linux, along with application development.

According to an IBM study of their customers, when Linux users were asked, "What's next for Linux deployment?" e-commerce applications were consistently number one or number two in the survey.

Add To, Don't Replace

Companies successfully using Linux view it as an *addition* to instead of *replacement* of their systems. Linux makes sense when adding new applications because your team can test on a

---

[47] www.sendmail.org
[48] www.samba.org

low-cost computer and move up to larger servers when it's time to roll out the project.

When you choose Linux, you strengthen your business by using your current computer investment more efficiently and get more bang for the buck when you buy new systems.

Business Applications

Linux is now increasingly being used for business applications such as e-commerce, accounting, retail, and finance. Other business application areas include enterprise resource planning (ERP), e-procurement, and customer relationship management (CRM). Ask your software vendor if they have your current business applications available to run under Linux. The odds are good that they do, or will soon.

Low-Cost Installations

Because Linux can run efficiently on less-powerful computers with limited memory and disk space, it's ideal for installations where cost is the prime consideration. For example, complete Linux-based computer systems can now be purchased new for about USD $300. These machines match or outperform faster computers running Windows.

Linux doesn't require a complete software installation for stable operation. A light-weight installation with just the components needed saves disk space and reduces memory requirements.

These types of systems work well for educational institutions, libraries, developing countries, and public-access systems.

Locked Systems and Thin Client Computing

Many businesses with high security requirements and compliance mandates want their systems locked to prevent employees from loading new programs, copying data, changing critical settings, or inadvertently introducing viruses.[49]

---

[49] A form of security breach called *social engineering* involves tricking an employee into loading a malicious program. For example, an employee finds a disk labeled "Executive Salaries" in the parking lot. Curi-

This environment demands a networked computer with limited local storage called a *thin client*.[50] Low in cost, these computers support a keyboard and display, accessing software and data storage from the local network. This lets the company completely control the business applications, data storage, and security. Users can view and change data on the screen, but little else.

Industries that require this level of security include banks and financial institutions, healthcare organizations, publicly-held companies, highly-competitive corporations, and anyone doing business in California.[51]

---

ous, they put it in their machine, open the files, and inadvertently infect their computer and any unsecured machine on the network.

[50] One of the leading companies in thin client technology is Citrix. www.citrix.com

[51] Concerned with ID theft, California's Database Security Breach Notification Act (SB1386) requires that customers be notified if a company believes a computer system's breach has compromised the personal information of any California customer.

Consolidating Server Farms

Server farms are typically rows and rows of interconnected UNIX- and Windows-based computers that provide a company with their data processing systems. These have proliferated over the past few years because individual servers are cheap. When a company needed more power or wanted to add a new application, they just plugged in another computer.

Server Farm Value Questioned

As server farms grew, companies discovered that they are complex to manage and maintain. Costs multiply because of increasing power and space requirements.

System reliability suffers because of the interdependence of the servers: if one goes down, others are affected. And as the server farm gets larger, the failure rates of the interdependent servers compound.[52] For example, if

---

[52] From statistics: reliability rate of the group equals the reliability of a single serve raised to the power of the number of servers in the group.

each server has a 99 percent reliability rate, two interdependent servers have 98 percent reliability as a group, four have 96 percent reliability, and 16 have 85 percent reliability.

Granted, most computers have a much higher reliability rate, yet the effect of compounding reliability diminishes server farm performance as they grow.

One Server, Many Applications

Until recently, businesses have often been locked into server farms because the applications they wanted required individual Windows or UNIX machines. Companies can consolidate server farms using a technology call *virtual machines*.[53] A single powerful computer looks like hundreds of smaller computers running a variety of OS's. Each virtual machine can run independent applications, delivering substantial savings of management requirements, power, and space.

---

[53] A leading supplier of this technology is VMWare. www.vmware.com

High Availability Computers

One way around the failure rate concerns of server farms is to use *clusters* of computers with fail-over systems to keep a single server's malfunction from seriously affecting the operation.[54] These clusters can create computing systems with very high availability, often talked about as 99.999 (five nines) percent availability or better. This means that the computer system is unavailable for fewer than nine hours per year, total.

Supercomputers

With Linux, businesses can build supercomputers out of low-cost standard Intel servers. Universities doing research, companies involved in life sciences, and businesses that need to quickly process massive amounts of data have adopted Linux supercomputer clusters.

---

[54] Two vendors of clustering software:
Steeleye Technology, Inc. www.steeleye.com
and Oracle. www.oracle.com

Clustering multiple systems together with the right software to create a supercomputer dramatically reduces the data processing start-up cost, increases reliability, and makes super-computing accessible to many more businesses. Clusters of computers running Linux rank in the top 10 of the world's largest supercomputers.[55]

Application Development

The flexibility, reliability, and cost-effectiveness of Linux make it a great platform for computer application developers. A substantial number of computer software companies now use Linux-based systems to create their software solutions.[56] One important reason is because Linux-based software runs on so many different computers without any modifications.

With open source development tools, your team can download tools and begin work immediately without worrying that the software

---

[55] www.top500.org

[56] One open source development tool organization is eclipse.org.

may stop working because the free-trial version or traditionally-licensed version expires.

Where Not to Use Linux

There are some places where you may elect not to use Linux. Most companies who have adopted Linux haven't abandoned other OS's. They simply use Linux where it makes the most sense and choose other OS's for other tasks.

Ask your independent IT consultant for a technology assessment of your company for the most accurate and relevant advice on where Linux makes sense and where it doesn't.

For each of the following situations, Linux works well for supplying network support services such as file and print servers.

Replacing Windows Desktops

If your people rely heavily on Windows-based tools , such as Microsoft Office, to get their jobs done at their desk, don't change the desk-top OS. While there are Linux-based alternatives to Office that satisfy some users' needs,[57] experi-

---

[57] See a list in the appendix on page 98.

enced users may not be pleased with them. This is especially true for power users who have developed macros and other application-based processes and procedures.

Some companies choose to offer Windows-based systems for power users, and Linux thin clients[58] for everyone else.

Running Windows Programs on Linux

WINE[59] is a Linux application that that makes Microsoft Windows-based software think that it's running on Windows. Xandros also makes a Linux desktop OS that supports many Windows programs.[60]

Microsoft XP licenses restrict running applications on anything other than the Windows OS. So if you run Office XP on WINE, you may be violating your Microsoft license agreement.

WINE is not 100 percent Windows compatible so test carefully if you want to run a Windows program under Linux.

---

[58] For more on thin clients, see on page 47.
[59] www.winehq.com
[60] www.xandros.com

OS-Specific Tools

Some tools have been developed for an OS to execute specific tasks. A good example: Mac OS 10 is well regarded for graphic arts, audio production, video editing, and photographic work. There aren't yet strong Linux-based programs that match the capabilities of these tools.

Custom Systems

A *legacy system* describes a computer application (often proprietary) that's important to daily operations, but that's so old, that it's expensive to maintain or the documentation is missing. The programs are usually written in older languages like COBOL and probably run on ancient hardware. Industry analyst, Gartner estimates that more than 70 percent of worldwide business applications are written in COBOL and that more than 180 billion lines of COBOL business code are in use.

You may not wish to replace your legacy system because of the business risk if the transition doesn't work well or because there isn't enough budget to rewrite the program. But you may wish to bring in new, more reliable hardware to improve speed, enhance security, implement a disaster recovery plan, or add new applications. A Linux-based server can deliver Web-based access to the old software or add more business functions without touching the original program. This is best left to an IT consultant with broad knowledge and experience with your type of computer systems.

Another solution comes from Acucorp[61] that provides software to run COBOL applications on Linux. They have relationships with BEA, HP, IBM, and others.

One more option is to look to the open source community. Members have developed ways to solve most problems integrating existing applications into a Linux environment. That's unique; most software vendors won't support unusual integration situations without hefty consulting fees.

---

[61] www.acucorp.com

How to Decide if Linux is Right for Your Company

The process of bringing Linux into your company is similar to bringing on any other new technology. It starts with reviewing where you want your company to go and identify the barriers to making that happen. Next, assemble a technology committee to craft strategic approaches to eliminating the barriers and evaluate potential solutions. Create smart questions that uncover the necessary information so that you can make intelligent choices, balancing risk and reward.

Company Direction

Deciding if Linux is right for your company requires you to assess where you are now and where you want to go and decide if the ROI meets your needs.[62] Consider these scenarios.

---

[62] See a list of ROI factors on page 40.

Growing

If your company is growing and you plan for your computer systems to expand, then the business case for Linux is sound.

Stable

If your company isn't growing or is growing slowly, you may wish to consider Linux to reduce computer system costs. You'll eliminate the annual license fees imposed by other OS vendors.

Retrenching

If your company is retrenching, you may want to keep the status quo to minimize retooling costs.

Merger or Acquisition

If you are planning to sell the company or merge in the near future, moving to Linux and open source software increases the ease of combining the computer systems.

Questions for Your Technology Committee

These questions let you examine your current computer systems to determine if using Linux or expanding Linux use makes sense.

What has been your experience with Linux? When was that?

If your team's experience is more than a few years old, recommend a review of current Linux releases before coming to a final conclusion.

Are you using Linux for individual fiel or print servers or Web servers? Why did your team decide to use Linux instead of other OS's?

These questions explore if your team uses Linux now and their rationales.

Who in the company is already comfortable with Linux?

Because of the compelling psychology of working with a community of fellow programmers, many software designers have learned Linux on their own. If your team has experience with Linux, this can be a good reason to standardize on this operating system for your computer servers. The person who's comfortable with Linux will have well thought out recommendations for the rest of your team.

Where are you using UNIX right now for network support such as file servers, print servers, e-mail servers, and Web servers?

Linux is a natural replacement for these types of applications, typically saving 30 to 70 percent in hardware, software, and administration costs.

For what applications are you considering a server upgrade or service expansion? What will it cost to do that? What will it cost to expand again?

Looking beyond a pending upgrade gives you a long-term view of the value of using Linux.

Where do you have leased UNIX computers and when do those leases expire?

Anytime that a computer lease expires, prudence demands that you review other technology options. Linux may be able to replace the leased systems at much lower cost.

What challenges have you experienced in the past with operating system upgrades? What has that cost in terms of installation costs, training, and lost productivity?

Most companies have lost productivity when upgrading operating systems, especially Windows. If you can get an idea of how much that disruption has cost your company, you can identify one possible source of ROI for a Linux-based solution.

What has been your experience with Windows' reliability on Intel-based servers?

Perhaps you can replace a limping Windows system with a Linux installation. You may wish to explore the business cost of unstable or unreliable servers.

What are your security risks? What is the plan to minimize them?

Every organization has been hit by viruses or by a hacker attack. Look at your risks, especially OS patching policies and access management. You may substantially secure your operation with a few important changes.

What are your challenges in managing and controlling your server farms?

If you have server farms now, they probably made sense when they were built. But they may make less sense now as mid-range hardware costs have come down. This opens the discussion to explore if consolidating servers is a reasonable business option.

Does your team feel locked in to one particular hardware or software vendor because of the operating system? How does that limit taking advantage of new or more cost-effective hardware?

These questions let you identify if lack of choice is an issue for your team. Vendor salespeople will try to lock you into their proprietary system. Determine if their recommendations are sound by getting a second, independent opinion. Find out what choosing proprietary systems means in potential ROI or current opportunity cost.

What applications do you have running on different OS's that use a different user interface? What is that inconsistency costing the organization?

Linux delivers a consistent user interface independent of the computer hardware. This question helps identify areas where interface consistency could make a difference in productivity.

Linux Adoption Strategy

Now that you've decided to move forward with Linux, you'll need to create an adoption strategy to make sure that you meet your business and budget goals. Creating a solid strategy is half the battle. Consider these best-practice concepts when formulating your strategy.[63]

Form a Corporate Standards Committee

Your standards committee can be your regular technology team or a subset that includes users from various departments. Your team needs to understand the issues of licensing, compliance, project selection, security, installation, testing, and rollout to formulate your corporate standards.

---

[63] For a good best-practices discussion aimed at the CIO, see news.com.com/2009-1069-982090.html

Standardize the Vendors

The number of Linux distributions and variety of Linux software may feel overwhelming, so how do you choose?

Prudent IT managers will evaluate Linux vendors, or any other software or hardware choice, in the context of what they need to accomplish. Approach your Linux installation as you would a commercial software installation balancing capability, support, and cost. You can get high-quality support for your Linux installations from vendors like Dell, HP, Oracle, and IBM.

Tens of thousands of IT consultants provide support for Linux and Linux-based programs. Many major software manufactures offer Linux versions of their software, including business-focused companies like IBM, Oracle, and SAP. It's quite likely that your present IT consultants and vendors can support Linux.

Because Linux is a flavor of UNIX, anyone with UNIX experience (or one of the common versions, such as Hewlett-Packard's HPUX or

IBM's AIX) will know 95 percent or more of what they need to support Linux.

Linux Certification

One indicator of a consultant's ability to deliver quality services is certification.

Most commercial software certification is administered by the vendor. But Linux certification, much like open source software, has no one company driving. There are competing Linux certifications available and the best known include the Red Hat Certified Engineer (RHCE), Linux Professional Institute (LPI), and Sair Linux and GNU Certification.

Red Hat[64] offers hands-on training and certification for their distribution. Their test includes demonstrating troubleshooting skills on Linux machines.

LPI[65] offers a vendor neutral certification focusing on the functions found in all Linux distributions and common tools. They offer

---

[64] www.redhat.com
[65] www.lpi.org

four levels of testing equivalent to junior though senior system administrator.

Sair[66] is part of the Thomson Learning family of training companies. Their Linux certifications cover the most popular distributions and are used by HP and other major corporations for training field engineers.

When reviewing consultant certifications, find out when they were first certified to get a feeling for their Linux experience and when they were last certified to understand how current they are with Linux.

Questions to Ask Your IT Vendor

Conduct standard due diligence when selecting a new vendor.

Tell me about your most recent Linux installation.

How long have you been supporting Linux?

What Linux installations have you worked with?

---

[66] www.linuxcertification.org

What's the training process for your IT consultants?

What certifications do you hold? When were you last certified?

What has been your experience in converting other OS installations to Linux?

Standardize the Linux

Select one Linux distribution vendor and stick with them. This simplifies system administration and the upgrade process.

Which Linux Distribution to Choose

No matter which distribution you choose, you'll end up with essentially the same kernel. There are differences in the installation procedures, the included tools and applications, and other technical differences.

Linux is available in local language versions that bundle together modifications and documentation required for that locality. A quick Internet search will turn up multiple Linux sources for supporting specific languages.

The most popular and best supported Linux distributions presented in alphabetical order:[67]

Nitix Linux is a distribution that self manages installation and operation, automating most server management tasks. Includes software for automating many network services. www.nitix.com

Mandrake Linux is very popular with new and home users. Installation is reportedly user-friendly, and it installs the KDE Windows-like graphical user interface. www.mandrakesoft.com

Red Hat Linux is the best-known distribution of Linux with more market share than all other distributors combined. It has a strong reputation for consistency and reliability mak-

---

[67] Caldera Linux would be on this list, but SCO withdrew it from distribution as of this writing.

ing it the de-facto standard in corporate America.
www.redhat.com

SUSE Linux is well supported by Novell. Novell's NetWare® was one of the top network operating systems, recently eclipsed by Linux. IBM funded Novell with USD $30 million based on their successful acquisition of SUSE Linux from its original German owner. www.suse.com

Turbolinux specializes in Linux distributions for Asia Pacific and offers strong support for desktops, servers, and larger computers. www.turbolinux.com

UnitedLinux is a consortium of four Linux distributors (of which, SCO, has withdrawn their distribution). The basic Linux kernel is the same and each distributor supplies their own tools, user interface, installation systems, documentation, and support. www.unitedlinux.com

Standardize the Servers

Simplify your IT budget and on-going operation by creating standard server configurations that handle your key applications.

Standardize the Procedures

With computer provisioning, management, and reporting tools (such as those from IBM, Oracle, and Veritas) your people can automate many computer maintenance tasks, like storage management, back up, software patch management, system configuration, and security audits. Tools like these can let an operator care for ten times as many servers.

Slowly Switch Standards

Choose a Linux project that has a limited effect on your company so your people can get up to speed. Then do a cost-cutting versus risk analysis to choose the next project.

Which Project to Choose First

Best practices dictate that you select a project for Linux and use that as the testing ground for your organization. It doesn't make sense to do a wholesale switch of all of your systems; too much is at stake.

One place to look is where your company is now running Windows NT4. Microsoft will soon be discontinuing support for this OS and you might explore Linux as a replacement, especially if the servers are used for file servers, print servers, mail, or Web servers.

Another place to look is where you have leased UNIX equipment that's about to expire. Linux may be able to replace the leased systems a much lower cost.

Applications and Success Stories

There are literally thousands of documented Linux case studies. Most Linux vendors offer loads of success stories in virtually every industry and application. If you're looking for specific applications in your industry, a quick Internet search will turn up many examples.

This section offers you a few examples of industries where Linux is successful.[68]

---

[68] See mtechit.com/linux-biz for a long list of corporations that use Linux along with their technical configurations.

Linux in Health Care

No matter where you are in the world, health care providers are under pressure to supply more services for less money. Add mandated security requirements and increasing demands for on-line medical records, and the business case for Linux becomes strong.

One clearinghouse for information about Linux healthcare applications can be found at www.linuxmednews.com.

Diagnostics Database

Open Source Clinical Application & Resources (OSCAR) delivers an online reference tool that improves critical diagnostic and therapeutic decisions made by medical practitioners. Running under Linux, the software pools patient data (stripped of personal details) from secure Web sites, worldwide. All patients participating in the research sign a consent form and understand how the data is used. Physicians can refer to treatment decisions made by other experts based on a patient's health profile.

Joseph Dal Molin, founder of the Open Source Health Care Alliance, reasons, "The open source approach is non-threatening... because it doesn't have any conflict of interest issues."[69]

National Mammography Archive

The University of Pennsylvania's National Digital Mammography Archive (NDMA™) is a Linux-based grid of hardware and software designed to electronically capture, manage, and distribute mammography images and data online. The system consolidates a patient's data so that test results can be evaluated with powerful tools including teleradiology, computer-aided diagnostics, and breast cancer screening. Physicians access patient images and reports within 90 seconds, versus days to months in the past.[70]

---

[69] www.itbusiness.ca/index.asp?theaction=61&lid=1&sid=54474&adBanner=eGovernment

[70] www.ibm.com/software/success/cssdb.nsf/CS/TKNC-5W42D9?OpenDocument&Site=linuxatibm

Decreasing Costs

"The National Health Service in Britain is considering ditching Microsoft software after a row over mounting licensing costs. Richard Granger, NHS IT director, has ordered a trial of a Linux-based system from Sun Microsystems as part of a £2.3 billion computer modernisation plan. 'If this solution were to prove effective we could save the NHS and the taxpayer many millions of pounds while at the same time using rich and innovative software technology,' says Granger. Charles Andrews, Sun Microsystem's public sector head, said licence cost savings would come to tens of millions of pounds directly. 'And we won't force people to upgrade computers and technology on a 2-3 year cycle either. Customers can upgrade when they need to,' he said." (*The Observer*, December 7, 2003)[71]

---

[71] observer.guardian.co.uk/business/story/0,6903,1101344,00.html

Linux in Finance and Banking

Financial services use Linux to consolidate applications running on multiple servers onto a single server. Because of legislated archiving requirements, Linux is a great choice for this industry.

Banking

The Dnister Bank in the Ukraine uses Intel-based servers. Half of the servers run Linux because of improved stability, flexibility, ease of use, and good support compared with other OS's. The system administrator plans to increase that to 70 percent in the near future.[72]

Managing Growth

One of Italy's oldest banks, Banca Carige operates in 12 regions and five international cities

---

[72] www.mandrakebizcases.com/modules.php?name=News&file=categories&op=newindex&catid=40

and is growing at nearly 15 percent a year. To keep this growth, managers look for ways to offer customers new services and explore methods to improve business efficiency.

Banca Carige uses both IBM z/OS to run legacy systems and Linux to take advantage of open systems. This reduces the bank's business risk and permits development of new services.

Giorgio Seronello, IT Director, explains: "As a bank, we provide services, so we cannot have an IT architecture that is geared solely towards internal systems. We wanted to introduce open systems for the future without abandoning our stable and powerful legacy systems. Resilience was also our aim – to develop a highly secure disaster recovery option."[73]

Brokerage Houses

Just about every U.S. brokerage house has deployed Linux. Morgan Stanley, CitiGroup,

---

[73] www.ibm.com/software/success/cssdb.nsf/CS/DNSD-5WXGGZ?OpenDocument&Site=linuxatibm

and e-Trade all run Linux to save money, simplify data center tasks, and take advantage of a consistent IT infrastructure. Many banks and insurers are considering following suit.[74]

Mortgage Companies

"In our business, we need the most stable platform available to communicate with our customers. Any downtime would cost thousands of dollars in expensive on-call staffing and potentially jeopardize our client relationships. ...Linux has helped us achieve 99.999 percent uptime," says First Network Mortgage CEO, Peter Domingue.

The company also decreased hardware costs and cut administrative time by 50 percent.[75]

---

[74] news.com.com/2030-1069_3-5059572.html
[75] www.suse.de/en/company/customer_references/finance.html

Mark S.A. Smith

Linux in Education

Educators always face the challenge of budget constraints and aging equipment. Many Linux vendors offer special educational discount programs to encourage Linux adoption.

Linux is ideal for educators because it operates well on older, less powerful computers and reduces system administration costs.

Efficient Student Workstations

Kyoto Sangyo University, Japan attracts students and faculty with its cutting-edge technology.

"Linux is becoming mainstream, and we wanted to host both (Windows NT and Linux) systems on a single server to make more efficient use of classroom space," says Nobuo Tsubouchi, head of operations at the University's Computer Center.

The University installed 1,725 IBM servers in a new six-story building and other engineering and science facilities. Every computer can be remotely refreshed every night with just a few mouse clicks. "This will minimize security and virus problems," said Tsubouchi.[76]

Information Portal

Technical University of Kaiserslautern, Germany created a central information portal and communication platform with e-mail, calendar, workflow, and document management functions for project participants. The result was more security and stability, reduced administration workload, and reduced price.[77]

Upgraded Databases for Less

The database at Vanderbilt University, Nashville, Tennessee, was growing at 1,000 percent per year and their computers weren't keeping up. An upgraded Intel and Linux solution cost 60 percent less than an equivalent mainframe solution. Plus, the UNIX skills of the staff rapidly transferred to Linux. Kevin McDonald,

---

[76] www.ibm.com/software/success/cssdb.nsf/CS/NAVO-59HPKM?OpenDocument&Site=linuxatibm

[77] www.suse.de/en/company/customer_references/all.html

Program Manager for System Administration says, "...(With Linux) we could get three times the server power and performance for the dollar, plus greater system availability."[78]

---

[78] www.redhat.com/solutions/info/casestudies/vanderbilt.html

Linux in Manufacturing

Linux delivers efficiencies and the long life cycle of hardware and software that manufacturing demands.

Use What You Have

Lip France is a small, boutique watch company with 30 employees. Their Linux-based e-mail system runs on an aging, low-cost computer system (Pentium II 200 MHz, 2.5 gigabyte disk and 96 megabyte of RAM). Because of the company size, there is no computer specialist, so the CEO updates accounts from his own PC if necessary. Otherwise, Linux allows the e-mail system to run unattended.[79]

Start Small

The Charnvel Group, Nottingham, England, manufacturers low voltage switchgear and

---

[79] www.mandrakebizcases.com/modules.php?name=News&file=categories&op=newindex&catid=54

control panels. The initial Linux installation was network services (Samba) for 10 people. Impressed with the stability and up-times, they have added Internet access, e-mail, intranet, groupware, and a database.[80]

Scale Up

Lithonia Lighting, one of the largest industrial and commercial lighting manufacturers in the world, uses technology to stay efficient and manage the wide range of products that they manufacture. Lithonia migrated from a single database server to clustered Linux servers. The result: lower costs and improved productivity.[81]

---

[80] www.mandrakebizcases.com/modules.php ?name=News&file=categories&op=newindex &catid=54

[81] www.redhat.com/solutions/info/casestudies/

Linux in Retail

Retail needs reliable systems. If the database systems fail, then inventory management systems don't work.

Linux is Open All the Time

McDonald's 1,200 restaurants in Germany use Linux. Thomas Trepl, McDonald's New Technologies Project Manage, says, "All in all, an enormous stability and availability is clearly evident. ...Linux has resulted in uptimes of more than 400 days, interrupted only due to extensions on the hardware side."[82]

More Stable Systems

Verweij Fashion in Amsterdam moved to Linux after Windows NT crashed several times a week. Functions provided by their Linux server include Internet connection and firewall,

---

[82] www.suse.de/en/company/customer_references/all.html

mail server, backup, intranet server, Samba file server, and other tools.[83]

Same Computers, More Capacity

Costco, Mexico needed to increase the traffic capacity of the Web site that serves their suppliers. The Linux version adds more capacity and requires half the processing power for the same traffic as their previous solution. Explains Omar Zamora, Manager of Systems of Costco: "Now we are using four servers with load balancing to obtain high availability."[84]

---

[83] www.mandrakebizcases.com/modules.php?name=News&file=article&sid=281

[84] www.suse.de/en/company/customer_references/costco.html

Linux in Transportation

Uptime

Robert Redford Shipping Agency located in Montreal and Toronto, Canada switched to Linux for better performance and no more computer crashes. "We have experienced 200-day uptimes on our PC workstations, an unheard of thing in the Windows world."[85]

Stability

As Global Transport Logistics clients came to expect real-time transactions 24 hours a day, computer systems needed to always be available. A move to Linux increased security, stability, and performance.[86]

---

[85] www.mandrakebizcases.com/modules.php ?name=News&file=article&sid=73

[86] www.mandrakebizcases.com/modules.php ?name=News&file=article&sid=290

Complex Logistics

The Clipper Group is a shipping consortium that controls approximately 250 vessels. Profitable shipping requires careful tracking to present an accurate account of each ship's bookings and capacity as it moves from port to port.

Clipper uses groupware running on Linux to update every agent's laptop with the latest shipping information and space availability status. Security and availability is a critical aspect of the implementation. Clipper chose Linux because it's non-proprietary and open.[87]

---

[87] www.ibm.com/software/success/cssdb.nsf/CS/ EHON-5S5PDL?OpenDocument&Site=linuxatibm

Linux in Entertainment

Entertainment companies demand efficiency, security, and near 100 percent up time. Linux delivers.

Supercomputers for Animation

Hollywood uses Linux server farms forming massive computers to create special effects and animation for a fraction of the cost of other methods. Animators choose Linux for its reliability, performance, ease of set-up, and substantially lower cost, up to a factor of ten cheaper.[88]

Costs Down, Capacity Up

In 2000, Weather.com, the online counterpart of Atlanta-based The Weather Channel Interactive Inc.'s 24-hour TV channel, relied on proprietary commercial software to serve up maps, forecasts and hour-by-hour weather data.

---

[88] www.computer.org/computer/homepage/0202/ec/

Today, the Web site runs almost entirely on open-source software and commodity hardware, slashing IT costs by one-third and increased Web site processing capacity by 30 percent as it serves up more than 50 million pages on stormy days.[89]

Stable and Reliable

Romance.UCam.org is a highly successful society for single members of Cambridge University, United Kingdom. The site's initial design used proprietary commercial software. It crashed weekly and the database was always corrupted. With a Linux implementation, the site almost runs itself. "The only interruptions we get are due to power outages!" says the Webmaster.[90]

Profits Sooner

SDRadio.net, a San Diego radio news site used open-source software to help turn a profit after

---

[89] opensource.org/weblog/2004/04/27#weatherdotcom
[90] www.mandrakebizcases.com/modules.php
?name=News&file=article&sid=413

18-months on line. Says the owner, "I wouldn't have had a positive cash flow if forced to upgrade to the latest [their words] 'greatest' OS and associated programs."[91]

---

[91] www.mandrakebizcases.com/modules.php?name=News&file=article&sid=200

Linux in Communications

Communications companies demand stability, security, long equipment life, and maximum value for the cost.

Cell Phone OS

Japanese manufacturer, NTT DoCoMo wants handset suppliers to slash costs by choosing Linux as the cell phone operating system.[92]

Frees Up Finds

EG Localisation, Brest, France, specializes in new IT and communication technology. A small company, they couldn't invest thousands of euros in proprietary computing systems with mediocre reliability and security. With the decreased costs of Linux, they freed up capital for the company's core activities."[93]

---

[92] www.nttdocomo.com
[93] www.mandrakebizcases.com/modules.php?name=News&file=article&sid=293

Competitive Product Development

CIRPACK, a voice switch developer in Suresnes, France, chose to base their SoftSwitch product on a Linux cluster because of high availability, resiliency, and dramatically reduced support costs. The result was a product that competes favorably with those from much larger telecom companies.

CIRPACK saw a four-fold increase in business in first 12 months because they could now sell into the high-end carrier market. Plus, with Linux open source software, customers can rapidly develop new services with the time to market being weeks instead of months.[94]

---

[94] www.ibm.com/software/success/cssdb.nsf/CS/ TKNC-5VA2KK?OpenDocument&Site=linuxatibm

Linux in Government

Governments aren't as influenced by market pressure when it comes to purchases when compared with other companies. They aren't forced to be efficient or competitive. Yet most governments try to do their best with what they have. Linux supplies lower costs and the long support life demanded by public records storage and retrieval.

Police Operations

Robert Shingledecker, the information systems manager for the city of Garden Grove, Calif., said the city's entire government, including 24-hour-per-day police department operations, has been running on Linux since 1995.[95]

Records Management

One point two million U.S. Army soldiers access their personnel records through the Web with the Army's Personnel Electronic Record

---

[95] www.shingledecker.org

Management System (PERMS). The Army chose Linux on Intel hardware for the Web server because of reduced costs and increased reliability.[96]

Supercomputer

The Department of Defense (DoD) High Performance Computing Modernization Program (HPCMP) uses a 2,132-processor Intel Linux cluster for the Army Research Laboratory Major Shared Resource Center (MSRC).[97]

Earlier Warning

U.S. National Weather Service officials use Intel workstations running Linux to reduce system processing time and maintenance costs. Meteorologists and hydrologists have the benefit of 400 percent faster processing speeds (when compared with older workstations) in

---

[96] www.redhat.com/solutions/info/casestudies/usarmy.html

[97] www.oss.gov.za/modules.php?op=modload&name=News&file=article&sid=113&mode=thread&order=0&thold=0

delivering severe weather watches and warnings.[98]

Cost Reduction

The Taiwanese government has launched a project to look into using Linux to save USD $295 million in royalty payments to Microsoft.[99]

---

[98] www.fcw.com/fcw/articles/2003/1208/web-nws-12-09-03.asp
[99] asia.cnet.com/newstech/systems/0,39001153,39145673,00.htm

Appendix A - Applications

This is a *very minor* sampling of software available for Linux. A cursory Web search will present you with many other options.

These are not recommendations, but a list of resources as a way for your team to get a jump start. Approach these companies with due diligence as you would with any new vendor.

Almost all programs are free or distributed under the GNU Library General Public License. Those that aren't free are usually a fraction of typical software licensing costs.

Office Suites

These packages compete with commercial products like Microsoft Office and bundle the various applications that most people need to conduct business.

KOffice

KOffice includes word processor, spreadsheet, database, flow charter, drawing, image editing, and presentation software. It can also run on several flavors of UNIX.
www.koffice.kde.org

OpenOffice

Includes word processor, spreadsheet, presentation manager and drawing program; open-source databases can be easily integrated. OpenOffice runs on Solaris, Linux, Windows, and Mac OS. It is sophisticated and flexible, working transparently with a variety of file formats, including Microsoft Office.
www.openoffice.org

Siag Office

A tightly integrated office package including a word processor, spreadsheet, text editor, animation program, file manager, and PostScript previewer. Siag Office can run on Linux, HP-UX, and other UNIX flavors. www.siag.nu

StarOffice

A commercial shrink-wrap package from Sun, this includes word processing, spreadsheet, presentation, drawing, and database capabilities. Versions are available for Linux, Solaris (Sun's UNIX flavor), and Microsoft Windows.
wwws.sun.com/software/star/staroffice/

Workplace

IBM offers server-based word processing, spreadsheet, and presentation software along with e-mail and instant messaging as part of their Lotus Workplace product. Workplace runs on Linux, UNIX, and operating systems used in handheld computers and cellular phones.
www.lotus.com/workplace

Groupware

E-mail communication and scheduling is the heart of the modern company, and strong groupware keeps that heart pumping. Here are a few companies that offer Linux-based products.

Communigate Pro

Communigate Pro is corporate email and groupware alternative to Microsoft's Exchange Server.

www.stalker.com

Evolution

Ximian (another Novell company) produces software for personal and workgroup information management running on Linux and UNIX-based systems. Evolution software integrates email, calendaring, meeting scheduling, contact management, and task lists.

www.ximian.com

InsightServer

Bynari offers an enterprise email server that scales from Intel platforms to IBM mainframes, providing world-class reliability for hundreds of thousands of users. www.bynari.net

Lotus Domino Express

This is IBM's industrial-strength software marketed to companies with one thousand or fewer employees. The IBM Express products let smaller companies tap the messaging and collaboration tools of Domino at lower prices. www.ibm.com

OpenExchange Server

OpenExchange from SUSE (a Novell company) offers tools needed for communication: e-mail server, Web server, groupware, collaboration, and messaging. www.suse.com

phpGroupWare

This free application provides a Web-based calendar, to-do list, address book, e-mail, news headlines, and a file manager. www.phpgroupware.org

Sendmail

Sendmail offers a complete line of email routing, storage, and access servers. Free version: www.sendmail.org. Commercial version: www.sendmail.com.

Appendix B - Useful Web Sites

These sites are a good starting point for Linux resources. A quick Internet search will give you many more options.

rootprompt.org

A clearinghouse for articles about UNIX operating systems. There are many reviews and articles about Linux and Linux-based business applications. Many of the articles get technical, yet this is a great site to find active Linux vendors.

www.linux.org

The official Linux Web site with lots of information for system administrators and developers. It also features a list of current Linux distributions.

www.about.linux.com

This site offers resources for larger companies using Linux, focusing on system administrators and developers.

www.linux.about.com

An extensive site targeting new users and PC-based Linux installations.

www.reallylinux.com

A Web site for Linux beginners including articles on getting started and transitioning from other PC-based systems.

searchenterpriselinux.com

Linux-specific information designed for IT professionals. Features executive-level articles about OS security and business applications.

About the Author

Mark S. A. Smith is an electrical engineer, computer programmer, hardware salesman, and software marketer who now works with clients to get more business out of their distribution channels.

After 22 years of working in and with high-tech sales and marketing channels, Mark identified that channel success depended on building value, driving demand, forming a powerful network, and protecting profits.

Mark focuses on how to rapidly create sound business decisions in a fast-paced business world. He delivers innovative, unconventional strategies for entrepreneurial thinkers, marketing managers, and sales professionals. Mark's an expert in creating instantly implementable tactics to achieve real business success.

Recognized by his peers, Mark is a full member of the Society for the Advancement of Consulting. Membership requires stringent proof of performance, expertise, and excellence in consulting. A veteran professional speaker, he is past president of the National Speakers Association, Colorado chapter.

He co-authored *Guerrilla Trade Show Selling*, *Guerrilla Teleselling*, and Guerrilla *Negotiating* with *Guerrilla Marketing* author, Jay Conrad Levinson, and *Guerrilla Selling* co-author, Orvel Ray Wilson.

He co-created the wildly successful Executive Assessment business case creation tool for IBM, writing approximately 70 product-specific versions for IBM's major software brands, including DB2®, WebSphere®, Lotus®, Tivoli®, and Start Now™.

Today he's president of Outsource Channel Executives, Inc, an organization that helps companies build sales channels and get more out the channels they have now. By uniquely combining product knowledge with sales and marketing skills, the company creates programs that instill excitement and confidence in people who have to sell.

Write him at Mark.Smith@OCEinc.com.

Index

Acucorp, 57
Amazon.com, 8, 38
Apache, 44
BEA, 57
blade servers, 20, 39
Bynari, 101
Caldera, 23, 70
Citrix, 19, 48
clusters, 51
COBOL, 56, 57
Communigate Pro, 101
Computer Associates, 19
Dell, 19, 21, 35, 66
Evolution, 101
Forrester Research, 43
Gartner, 10, 56
GNU, 13, 67, 98
groupware, 85, 89, 100, 101, 102
Hewlett-Packard, 8, 20, 21, See HP
high availability, 51
HP, 19, See Hewlett-Packard
IBM, 8, 11, 12, 19, 20, 22, 25, 26, 35, 45, 57, 66, 67, 71, 72, 79, 81, 100, 101, 106
IBM Express, 102
IDC, 10
Intel, 24, 34, 38, 51, 62, 78, 82, 96, 101
IT consultant, 54, 57
kernel, 12, 22, 37, 71
KOffice, 18, 99
legacy system, 56
Lotus Workplace, 100
mainframe, 34, 35, 82

Mandrake, 70
Microsoft, 8, 11, 19, 28, 36, 55, 73, 77, 97, 98, 100, 101
Microsoft Office, 18, 21, 54, 99
Munich, 22
Network Associates, 20
Nitix, 70
Novell, 20, 71, 101, 102
Open source, 14
OpenExchange, 102
OpenOffice, 18, 99
Oracle, 8, 20, 51, 66, 72
PeopleSoft, 20
phpgroupware, 102
POSIX, 11, 17
Red Hat, 20, 67, 70
ROI, 40, 58, 62, 64
Sair, 67, 68
Samba, 45, 85, 87

SAP, 20, 66
SCO, 11, 22, 23, 70, 71
sendmail, 44, 45, 102
Server farms, 49
Siag Office, 99
social engineering, 47
Stallman, Richard, 13
StarOffice, 18, 21, 100
Steeleye Technology, Inc, 51
Sun, 8, 20, 21, 35, 77, 100
supercomputer, 52
supercomputers, 11, 51, 52
SUSE, 71
SUSE LINUX, 21
TIVO, 9, 14

Torvalds, Linus, 12
Trend Micro, 20
Turbolinux, 71
UnitedLinux, 20, 71
UNIX, 8, 12
Veritas, 20, 72
virtual machine, 50
VMWare, 20, 50
Wal-Mart, 21

Windows, 8, 19, 22, 24, 28, 31, 36, 45, 47, 49, 50, 54, 55, 62, 70, 73, 86, 88, 99, 100
WINE, 55
X, 36
Xandros, 55

Notes

Notes

Notes

Notes

Notes

Notes